BIOINDICATOR SPECIES

CORAL REEFS
MATTER

by Julie Murphy

Content Consultant
Richard B. Aronson
Department of Biological Sciences
Florida Institute of Technology

Core Library

An Imprint of Abdo Publishing
abdopublishing.com

abdopublishing.com

Published by Abdo Publishing, a division of ABDO, PO Box 398166, Minneapolis, Minnesota 55439. Copyright © 2016 by Abdo Consulting Group, Inc. International copyrights reserved in all countries. No part of this book may be reproduced in any form without written permission from the publisher. Core Library™ is a trademark and logo of Abdo Publishing.

Printed in the United States of America, North Mankato, Minnesota
082015
012016

Cover Photo: Rostislav Ageev/Shutterstock Images
Interior Photos: Rostislav Ageev/Shutterstock Images, 1; iStockphoto, 4, 6, 8, 28, 43, 45; National Oceanic and Atmospheric Administration, 10; Ethan Daniels/Shutterstock Images, 12, 16; Reuters/HO/Greenpeace/Corbis, 14; Caters News/ZumaPress/Newscom, 21; Richard Whitcombe/Shutterstock Images, 22; Sandra Gätke/DPA/Corbis, 26; Reuters/HO/Greenpeace/ Corbis, 30; Wilfredo Lee/AP Images, 34; David Doubilet/National Geographic Creative/Corbis, 36; Udo Weitz/EPA/Corbis, 38; Jurgen Freund/Nature Picture Library/Corbis, 40

Editor: Jon Westmark
Series Designer: Laura Polzin

Library of Congress Control Number: 2015945396

Cataloging-in-Publication Data
Murphy, Julie.
 Coral reefs matter / Julie Murphy.
   p. cm. -- (Bioindicator species)
 ISBN 978-1-68078-009-3 (lib. bdg.)
 Includes bibliographical references and index.
 1. Coral reefs--Juvenile literature. 2. Coral reef ecology--Juvenile literature.   3. Environmental protection--Juvenile literature.   I. Title.
 577.7--dc23
                                                                            2015945396

CONTENTS

WHAT IS A CORAL REEF?

Life surrounds a bright, colorful reef in shallow waters off the coast of Australia. Fish of all sizes swim in and around the seafloor structures. Plantlike organisms stretch upward from what look like giant rocks. But the structures are not rocks. They too are living organisms. They are called corals. Corals do not have noticeable body parts, such as

Corals can come in many shapes, colors, and sizes.

Coral polyps use tentacles to catch tiny floating organisms.

faces or stems. But a single piece of coral is made of thousands of creatures, called polyps.

A Closer Look

Coral polyps have soft bodies that measure from 0.04 to 0.1 inches (0.1–0.3 cm) across. Tentacles around their mouths sting and grab tiny organisms that drift past.

Each polyp protects itself by sitting in a shell-like cup called a calyx. The polyp stretches the top of its body out of the calyx. This is how it feeds. The creature goes into the cup for protection if danger approaches.

The polyp builds its cup from calcium carbonate. This is also known as limestone. Limestone makes coral reefs look and feel stony. It also gives reef-building corals their name: hard corals.

How Coral Grows

As old polyps die in a coral reef, their soft bodies go away. But their cups remain. Over time, new polyps grow over the empty calyxes. This is how a coral reef grows. Over thousands of years, layers of new polyps settle on top of layers of old calyxes. This means only the outer layer of a coral reef is alive. The rest is made of empty cups.

Corals grow at different speeds. The rate depends on the type of coral and the conditions. Different types of reef-building corals grow into a

Hard corals grow in thick colonies, which eventually form reefs.

range of shapes and sizes. They may look like tables, mushrooms, branches, or fingers.

An Unusual Partnership

Polyps are not the only living things in coral. Each polyp contains algae. Algae are tiny, single-celled plants. The algae in coral are called zooxanthellae.

Coral polyps and their algae have a mutualistic relationship. This means both creatures benefit from living together. The algae get protection from the polyp's hard cup. They also use the polyp's waste. The algae turn the waste into food. They do this through a process called photosynthesis.

PERSPECTIVES
Parrot Fish

Parrot fish eat seaweeds living on coral reefs. To do this, they break the limestone framework of the reef using their parrot-like beaks. Special teeth in their throats crush the coral rock into powder. Parrot fish help corals by removing competing plants. But the fish also erode reefs and produce sand.

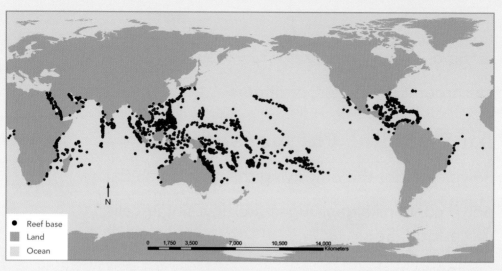

The World's Coral Reefs
Examine where the world's coral reefs are found. What do these places have in common?

Photosynthesis is powered by sunlight. It only occurs during the day.

The polyps benefit from the relationship in other ways. They use food and oxygen the algae make during photosynthesis. The polyps get important nutrients from the algae that they do not get from eating other animals.

The see-through polyps take on their guests' striking colors. Millions of algae give color to a single square inch (6 sq cm) of coral.

Where Are Coral Reefs Found?

Coral polyps need food from algae to live. And algae need sunlight to make food. So reefs are found in shallow, light-rich waters. Coral reefs also need warmth to grow. They prefer water temperatures from 73 to 84 degrees Fahrenheit (23–29°C). Corals need gentle waves to bring in nutrients and take away waste. Reefs also need to attach to solid ground. Coral reefs live in waters where all these needs are met.

Types of Reefs

Coral reefs come in many forms. The most common are fringing reefs. These reefs occur fairly close to shore. In the United States, they grow along the shallow waters of the southeast coast. Here they stretch for 358 miles (576 km). Barrier reefs also run alongside coastlines. But they are separated from land by deep water. Australia's Great Barrier Reef is the world's biggest reef. It is 1,429 miles (2,300 km) long. It can even be seen from space. Donut-shaped reefs are known as atolls. These form when a volcano sinks beneath the sea, leaving just its coral edges. Many atolls in the Indian and Pacific Oceans have coconut trees growing on them.

Coral polyps lose all their vivid colors when stressed.

Coral reefs grow in 109 countries, including the United States, India, Australia, and the Philippines. Most reefs are small and patchy. In total they cover less than 0.015 percent of Earth's oceans. This is an area slightly bigger than Texas.

What Is Happening to Coral Reefs?

Coral reefs need water that is shallow, clear, and gently moving. If any of these factors change, the temperature may change. This stresses corals. When stressed, algae may leave their polyps. They take their food production and bright colors with them. The coral then turns white, stops growing, and begins to starve. This action is called coral bleaching.

A coral reef is so sensitive to changes in water temperature that scientists use it as a bioindicator. A bioindicator is a living thing that is used to measure the health of an ecosystem. An ecosystem includes all the plants and animals living in the area. It also includes their interactions and the environment. The coral reef is just one part of its ecosystem. If water conditions change, coral bleaching is one of the first effects people see. It shows that the health of the ecosystem is going down.

If coral is stressed for just a short period, algae may come back. The coral can recover. But if the stress goes on for longer than six to eight weeks, the algae do not return and the coral dies.

Coral colonies do not necessarily bleach all at once. The process can move slowly through an area.

The first worldwide study of coral bleaching occurred in 1998. It found that more than half of reefs were at risk. Since then more than one quarter have died. Sixteen percent died in a mass bleaching event in 1998. The event was caused by a long, very warm season. Eleven percent were killed by other human impacts. These included pollution, overfishing, tourism, and mining.

EXPLORE ONLINE

Chapter One describes coral and how coral reefs form. The website listed below also talks about this. As you know, no two sources are the same. How is the information from the website the same as the information in Chapter One? What new information did you learn from the website?

National Geographic: Coral
mycorelibrary.com/coral-reefs-matter

THREATS TO CORAL REEFS

Coral reefs become stressed and die for many reasons. Natural events have been damaging reefs for millions of years. They include earthquakes, volcanic eruptions, and hurricanes. Today coral reefs face new threats caused by people. Two major threats are climate change and pollution.

Coastal pollution can introduce harmful substances into the ocean and hurt corals.

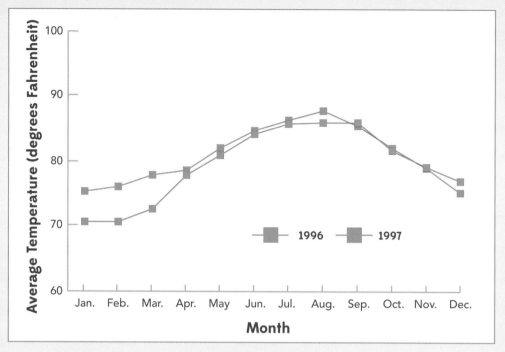

El Niño

Every three to eight years, ocean temperatures warm. The event is known as El Niño. From 1997 to 1998, a severe El Niño bleached huge amounts of coral reefs. The chart shows the difference in surface temperature between 1996 and 1997 in waters off the coast of Florida. What differences do you notice between the two years? How does the chart help you understand how sensitive coral reefs are to warming?

Climate Change

Climate change is caused by rising levels of greenhouse gases. These gases trap heat in the atmosphere. One of the most common greenhouse gases is carbon dioxide. It is released when people burn fuels, such as oil and gasoline. The result is a warming atmosphere. Earth's climate has naturally changed throughout history. But human actions are now causing it to change more quickly.

Climate change warms the air. Warmer air warms oceans too. Corals become stressed when water warms too much for too long. If water temperatures do not quickly return to normal, corals lose their algae and die.

In 1997 and 1998, water temperatures in the Pacific Ocean rose to dangerous levels. Bleaching lasted for approximately five months. The warm water made some reefs lose as much as 90 percent of their live coral. Bleaching events have occurred every year since.

As air warms, Earth's major ice masses slowly melt and flow into the ocean. The water in the ocean also expands as it gets warmer. These two things cause sea levels to rise. The reefs become farther from the surface as the water deepens. Corals receive less light. This slows photosynthesis, resulting in less food.

Seas have risen by approximately 0.13 inches (3.3 mm) per year over the past 20 years. So far this rise has not hurt reefs. Many have grown faster than the sea level has risen. But coral growth may slow in the future as other problems increase. And seas may rise faster.

With more greenhouse gases in the air, oceans take in more carbon dioxide. The gas dissolves into water. When this happens, the water's acidity goes up. With more acidic water, corals cannot take in enough calcium carbonate. Without this mineral, corals cannot build their hard cups.

Scientists do not agree on all the details about how climate change will affect weather patterns in the future. But models do predict some general trends. One possibility is that warmer air will cause more frequent intense storms. Storms can break and move coral. A big cyclone struck Australia in 2011. It brought winds of up to 177 miles per hour (285 km/h). Approximately six percent of the Great Barrier Reef was badly damaged.

Cyclone Yasi moves toward the Australian coast in 2011. The storm caused severe damage on land and in the sea.

Coastal Development

Approximately 44 percent of the world's population lives within 93 miles (150 km) of the ocean. People living near the ocean can bring harmful substances to it. Fertilizers, pesticides, and oil can hurt corals. Trash

Plastic bags and other debris can smother coral.

can bring poisons into coastal waters. And wildlife, such as turtles, may choke on debris or get tangled in it.

Sewage can hurt reefs indirectly. Nutrient-rich waste released into the sea promotes seaweed growth. This growth blocks light from getting to corals. It can slow or stop photosynthesis within corals.

Coastal Industries

People have fished the seas for thousands of years using nets, traps, lines, spears, and boats. At one time, the sea's supplies seemed limitless. Today modern fishing methods help people catch more fish than ever before. This can lead to overfishing. Overfishing is when so many fish are caught the remaining fish cannot restore the population. More than 80 percent of Earth's shallow reefs are overfished.

Crown-of-Thorns Starfish

Crown-of-thorns starfish eat coral. Since 1970 the starfish has sometimes become so great in number that it has eaten big sections of reefs. People are likely the main cause. Overfishing and pollution have removed many of the fish, shrimp, and worms that normally eat young crown-of-thorns starfish. Adult crown-of-thorns starfish are spiny and poisonous. They are hard to get rid of. To do so, each of the animals must be taken away one by one or injected with poison.

Overfishing near coral reefs does not just affect the fish species being caught. Changing numbers of fish can upset the balance of the whole ecosystem. For example, researchers in Kenya found that removing fish led to a big increase in the number of sea urchins. The sea urchins then ate the coral skeletons on the reef. The skeletons had given young corals a place to grow. Without these places, fewer young corals grew.

People do not only fish for food. Some catch fish to keep in aquariums. An estimated 2 million people worldwide keep tropical fish. Some people use explosives or chemicals to stun and catch these fish. These things can hurt many animals, including corals.

Overwhelmed

Coral reefs have shown an ability to recover from natural pressures. But different threats can combine to become too much for reefs. For example, corals already weakened by poor water quality are more likely to die from disease. Human actions can cause corals to be unable to recover from natural threats.

FURTHER EVIDENCE

Chapter Two describes reasons why Earth's coral reefs are in danger. What is the cause of most of the threats? What examples support this point? Read the information shown on the website below. How does the information on the website support the chapter's information? What new evidence does it present?

Coral Reef Threats

mycorelibrary.com/coral-reefs-matter

CHAPTER THREE

WHY CORAL REEFS MATTER

In 2000 scientists estimated 27 percent of Earth's reefs had been lost. Many countries have since taken action. They set aside reefs to be protected from things like fishing and boating. Yet not everyone is acting to care for the remaining coral. More than 40 countries have not set up any protections. This may lead to big problems for both reefs and humans.

Rangers in the Philippines paddle away from a watchtower. The rangers watch for illegal activity around the country's coral reefs.

The humphead wrasse is one of many species threatened by habitat loss and overfishing.

Environmental Consequences

Coral reef ecosystems are home to millions of types of animals and plants. Seahorses, lobsters, turtles, and giant clams are just a few examples of animals that need reefs to survive. More than one-quarter of all known fish species live near reefs.

Each species living around a coral reef has adapted to certain conditions over thousands of years. Without these settings, a species may not survive. One example is the humphead wrasse. This reef fish grows to around 6.5 feet (2 m) long. It is now endangered because of overfishing and habitat loss.

People have not been able to breed the fish outside the ocean. Without its original habitat, the humphead wrasse's future is in doubt.

Bleaching corals show scientists that reef habitats are suffering. Other ocean ecosystems are connected to coral reefs. Plants and animals in these ecosystems may also be affected over time.

Financial Costs

Coral reefs bring money and jobs to communities. Millions of people visit the coral reefs in southeast Florida each year. These reefs bring in approximately $2 billion per year and create more than 70,000 jobs to the local economy. Without coral reefs, communities that depend on reefs would suffer.

Many communities rely on reefs as barriers. Reefs keep land from being washed away by waves and floods. If these communities lose their reefs, storms could damage beaches, cities, and farms along the coast.

Barrier reefs absorb energy from waves. This helps protect coastlines from erosion.

Approximately 100 million people live within 6 miles (10 km) of a reef and 33 feet (10 m) from sea level. Reefs have been shown to lower wave height by 84 percent. If reefs are lost, nearby communities will need to build seawalls to protect their coasts.

Medical Effects

Coral reefs are a rich source of chemicals. Some can become useful substances, including medicines. Ara-C is one example. This medicine was created from a Caribbean reef sponge. It has helped save millions of people suffering from cancer. Many life-saving discoveries could be lost along with reefs.

Traditional Owners

Australia's aboriginal and islander people are the traditional owners of the Great Barrier Reef. Their families have been using its resources for more than 8,000 years. These communities still share the food they hunt and gather from the reef. The Great Barrier Reef is also important to these people in other ways. Communities still express myths and legends of the sea through dances, songs, and stories.

Coral Reef Restoration

People have been trying to help damaged reefs in a number of ways. Artificial reefs have been built. Damaged reefs have been held in place with pieces of dead coral. Living corals have been brought in to help suffering reefs. These methods are often difficult and expensive. They also take a very long time. Regrowing reefs can take hundreds of years. Future research must focus on what is causing the damage. This helps ensure regrowth is possible.

A Changing World

Reefs must be healthy to keep providing benefits to people. Scientists cannot test water quality everywhere or all the time. But they know the environment is becoming less healthy when they see coral changing. Reefs have shown they can recover with time. But the more problems reefs face, the harder a comeback becomes. It is important to listen to the signals coral reefs are giving. Doing so may allow us to change the trend of coral loss.

Scientists are finding new chemicals in and around coral reefs. In the following excerpt from *Issues in Science and Technology*, a scientist describes how reefs may yield useful products:

> *Coral reefs represent an important and as yet largely untapped source of natural products with enormous potential as pharmaceuticals, nutritional supplements, enzymes, pesticides, cosmetics, and other novel commercial products. The prospect of finding a new drug in . . . coral reef species, may be 300 to 400 times more likely than . . . from a terrestrial ecosystem. . . . Many [species] engage in a form of chemical warfare . . . to deter predation, fight disease, and prevent overgrowth. . . . Because of their unique structures or properties, these compounds may yield life-saving medicines or other important industrial and agricultural products.*
>
> Source: Andrew W. Bruckner. "Life-Saving Products from Coral Reefs." Issues in Science and Technology *Spring 2002. Print. 39.*

What's the Big Idea?

Read this text carefully. What is its main idea? How is the main idea supported by details?

CHAPTER FOUR

THE FUTURE OF CORAL REEFS

Protecting the world's reefs will require
management. People need to protect reefs
while also allowing their ongoing use. Marine
Protected Areas (MPAs) are one way managers try
to achieve this balance. MPAs are areas set aside
to preserve ocean habitat. Some areas ban things
like fishing for a length of time. Others allow fishing

Researchers survey corals in a Marine Protected Area. Scientific
studies help managers make good decisions for the area.

The goliath grouper became a protected species in 1990. These huge fish were nearly fished to extinction and are still recovering.

but do not allow other activities, such as oil drilling. Approximately one-fifth of Earth's reefs are in MPAs.

Florida Keys National Marine Sanctuary

In 1990 the Florida Keys National Marine Sanctuary was made an MPA. It features the world's third-largest barrier reef. It also includes more than 6,000 types of plants and animals and historically important shipwrecks.

Research keeps track of water quality, changes in marine life, and the role of people in causing these changes. Scientists study all the sanctuary's ecosystems, including its reefs. This helps them understand how the ecosystems are connected. This information helps managers make good decisions about how to protect the environment.

Managers must weigh many options. They must consider what is best for the environment and for the people visiting it. Visitors to the Florida Keys National Marine Sanctuary

Tourists in Thailand stand on living corals. Contact from humans can significantly harm corals.

are allowed to fish, dive, swim, and snorkel in some places. But these activities are monitored. Officers patrol the area to make sure visitors follow the rules. Penalties for breaking the rules range from a warning to a big fine. Educational programs tell visitors why the rules are important.

Reefs are managed in different ways around the world. Some are managed by communities. Others are managed privately. Many coral reefs are managed by governments. This is the case for the Florida Keys National Marine Sanctuary. Here the National Oceanic and Atmospheric Administration makes the final decisions.

A Global Effort

Each country is responsible for looking after its own reefs. These governments need access to current information. The data allows them to make good management decisions. This is where global organizations can help. The International Coral Reef Action Network (ICRAN) is one example. ICRAN was formed in 2000 with help from the United Nations Foundation. ICRAN links leading scientists with reef managers. It helps them exchange information. Better-informed managers are then able to oversee more helpful conservation.

There is still much work to be done. Some coral reef areas have more than one group in charge of reef protection. In these places, cooperation and communication need to be better. Managers could benefit from more training. And more public education is needed.

A diver lowers an artificial structure toward the seafloor to help coral regrow in the Philippines.

Worldwide cooperation is important too. Climate change is a threat to all coral reefs. It is a global problem. So the solution must also be global. This means we all have a part to play.

The loss of coral reefs tells us a lot about the effects of pollution, fishing, tourism, and climate change. Learning from these messages will help us preserve the world's reefs for the future. It will also help us save many other habitats from becoming threatened.

Declaring a reef as a Marine Protected Area does not ensure its protection. The following excerpt from a handbook on ocean ecosystems explains why:

> There are many problems with the management of [Marine and Coastal Protected Areas] in Asia. Although many MCPAs have been designated by governments and exist on "paper," management "on the ground" is often weak, and thus MCPAs fail to achieve their objectives. There are many reasons for this, including: a lack of government, human, or financial resources to manage these areas; poor enforcement and lack of support from enforcement authorities; lack of proper participation by local communities due to poor management design and failure to include people effectively; and corruption.

Source: Vineeta Hoon et al. "A Teacher's Toolkit for Investigating Coastal and Marine Ecosystems in Asia." ICRAN, 2008. Web. Accessed June 15, 2015.

Back it Up

The author of this text is using evidence to support a point. Write a paragraph describing the point the author is making. Then write down two or three pieces of evidence the author uses to make the point.

Common Name: Hard coral

Scientific Name: Scleractinia

Polyp Size: 0.04 to 0.1 inches (0.1–0.3 cm)

Color: Variety of colors, but mostly greens and browns

Average Life Span: 15 to 30 years

Diet: Plankton, fish, shrimp

Habitat: Shallow, tropical waters

Predators: Starfish, puffer fish, parrot fish, and snails

What's Happening: Algae in coral polyps are leaving due to changing environmental conditions. This causes coral bleaching.

Where It's Happening: Coral reefs around the world

Why It's Happening: Changes in water quality and temperature due to climate change, coastal development, and coastal industries

Why It's Important: Coral reefs produce many benefits: They help stop the erosion of coasts. They help maintain the world's rich diversity of animal and plant

species. They provide millions of people with food and income and are a major tourist attraction.

What You Can Do:

- Do not touch corals while diving.
- Do not buy souvenirs made of coral or marine animals.
- Choose eco-friendly resorts and tour operators.
- At home do not use chemical fertilizers or pesticides in your garden.
- Support organizations that protect corals reefs.
- Buy seafood products that come from a sustainable source.

Tell the Tale

Chapter Two discusses how a coral reef is part of an ecosystem containing a large community of plants and animals. Imagine you are snorkeling in Australia's Great Barrier Reef. Write 200 words about the animals and plants you encounter. How could you avoid harming the ecosystem?

Surprise Me

Chapter One discusses what a coral is. After reading this chapter, what two or three facts about corals and coral reefs did you find most surprising? Write a few sentences about each fact. Why did you find each fact surprising?

Dig Deeper

After reading this book, what questions do you still have about why coral reefs are threatened? With an adult's help, find a few reliable sources that can help you answer your questions. Write a paragraph about what you learned from your research.

Take a Stand

Chapter Four discusses how managers use Marine Protected Areas (MPAs) to try to strike a balance between protecting the environment and meeting the needs of the people who use the area. Do you think everyone has a right to do activities, such as fishing and snorkeling, in an MPA? Why or why not?

GLOSSARY

bleaching
when algae living inside coral leave because of stress

calyx
the cup-shaped shell of a coral polyp

ecosystem
a community of living things that affect one another and their environment

greenhouse gas
a substance in the air that traps heat in the atmosphere

management
controlling the impact of people on the environment

mutualism
a relationship between two species in which both benefit

overfishing
when so many of a particular fish species are taken from an area that the population's future is threatened

photosynthesis
the process by which plants use sunlight to make food

polyp
the animal whose colonies make up coral reefs

zooxanthellae
algae that live inside coral polyps

LEARN MORE

Books

Gagne, Tammy. *Coral Reef Ecosystems.*
Minneapolis, MN: Abdo Publishing, 2016.

Johnson, Robin. *Oceans Inside Out.* New York:
Crabtree Publishing, 2015.

Pyers, Greg. *Biodiversity of Oceans and Seas.* New
York: Marshall Cavendish Benchmark, 2012.

Websites

To learn more about Bioindicator Species, visit
booklinks.abdopublishing.com. These links are
routinely monitored and updated to provide the most
current information available.

Visit **mycorelibrary.com** for free additional tools for
teachers and students.

INDEX

ABOUT THE AUTHOR

Julie Murphy is a trained zoologist and a zookeeper. She has written numerous children's books about animals and the environment. Julie lives in Melbourne, Australia, with her husband, daughter, and two scruff-ball guinea pigs.